★ CONTENTS ★

P9-APY-630

Chester Arthur

Chester Arthur was the twenty-first US president. He got the position after President James A. Garfield was **assassinated**. Garfield had served just six months as president. Arthur had been his vice president.

Before becoming president, Arthur had not spent much time in politics. After college, he worked as a lawyer. In one famous case, he helped a group of slaves win their freedom. Arthur's success in court helped him gain the respect of many important people.

Arthur had never held an elected office until he became vice president in March 1881. President Garfield died the night of September 19 that year. Arthur took the oath of office on September 20. This made him the nation's leader.

President Arthur was an honest and hardworking man. He fought dishonest government workers. As president, Arthur made advancements to the country. He signed the first **civil service** law. And, he modernized and expanded the US Navy. These efforts helped Arthur win the country's respect.

TIMELINE

1829

On October 5, Chester Alan Arthur was born in Fairfield, Vermont.

1854

Arthur became a lawyer.

1859

On October 25, Arthur married Ellen Lewis Herndon.

1861

The American Civil War began.

1853

Arthur became Erastus D. Culver's apprentice.

1856

Arthur started his own law practice in New York City, New York.

1862

New York governor Edwin D. Morgan appointed Arthur New York quartermaster general.

1871

President Ulysses S. Grant made Arthur the collector of the New York customhouse.

1882

Congress approved improvements to the US Navy. Arthur signed the Chinese Exclusion Act. The Edmunds Anti-Polygamy Act passed.

1883

Arthur signed the Pendleton Civil Service Act. Congress lowered tariffs.

1880

On January 12, Ellen Arthur died of pneumonia.

1881

Arthur became James A. Garfield's vice president on March 4. On July 2, Charles Guiteau shot Garfield. President Garfield died on September 19. On September 20, Arthur became the twenty-first US president.

1886

On November 18, Chester Arthur died.

JAMES A. GARFIELD
REPUBLICAN CANDIDATE FOR PRESIDENT

CHESTER A. ARTHUR
REPUBLICAN CANDIDATE FOR VICE PRESIDENT

"Men may die, but the fabrics of our free institutions **remain unshaken.**"

CHESTER ARTHUR

DID YOU KNOW?

★ Before moving into the White House, President Chester Arthur had it cleaned and refurnished. Twenty-four wagonloads of rugs, furniture, and other belongings were hauled out. A new bathroom and new plumbing were installed, and the house was redecorated. Arthur finally moved in on December 7, 1881.

★ On May 24, 1883, President Arthur attended the opening of the Brooklyn Bridge in New York. At the time, it was the longest bridge in the world.

★ Abraham Lincoln's son Robert Todd Lincoln served as President Arthur's secretary of war.

★ On February 21, 1885, President Arthur dedicated the Washington Monument in Washington, DC.

★ Author Mark Twain published two books during Arthur's presidency. *Life on the Mississippi* came out in 1883. *Adventures of Huckleberry Finn* was published in 1885.

Young Chester

Chester Alan Arthur was born in Fairfield, Vermont, on October 5, 1829. The Arthur family was large. Chester had six sisters and two brothers.

William Arthur, Chester's father, was a Baptist minister. He had moved to America from Northern Ireland when he was a young man. Chester's mother, Malvina Stone Arthur, was from Vermont. She cared for the family.

The Arthurs were a close and loving family. William and Malvina read and prayed with their children. And, they made sure their children were educated. By age 15, Chester knew Latin and Greek.

William's job kept the family moving often. In 1839, they settled in Union Village, New York. Chester went to school in Union Village.

William Arthur

FAST FACTS

BORN: October 5, 1829

WIFE: Ellen Lewis Herndon (1837–1880)

CHILDREN: 3

POLITICAL PARTY: Republican

AGE AT INAUGURATION: 51

YEARS SERVED: 1881–1885

VICE PRESIDENT: none

DIED: November 18, 1886, age 57

Union College was founded in 1795.

Then in 1844, the family moved to Schenectady, New York. There, Chester entered Union College at age 15. One year later, he took on a part-time teaching job.

Chester was a good student. In just three years, he graduated from Union College near the top of his class! After graduation, Chester continued teaching while studying law.

Civil Rights Lawyer

Arthur's parents had taught him to treat people with **respect.** William was an abolitionist. So, he spoke out against slavery. Arthur shared his father's views on this important issue. He wanted to do something to end slavery.

Leading abolitionist lawyer Erastus D. Culver belonged to William's church. He agreed to train Arthur in his office. So in 1853, Arthur became Culver's **apprentice**.

Arthur helped Culver on the famous *Lemmon* slave case. This case involved Jonathan Lemmon and his wife. In 1852, they had taken eight slaves from Virginia to New York. New York did not allow slavery. So, the slaves wanted their freedom.

Lemmon refused to free the slaves. He did not believe New York's law applied to them. But Judge Elijah Paine Jr. disagreed with Lemmon. He granted the slaves their

Elijah Paine Jr.

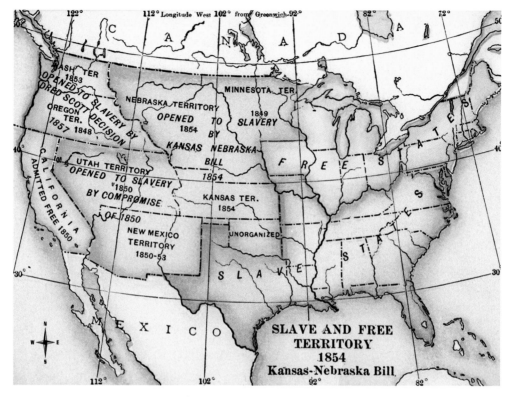

Map showing the slave and free areas of the United States in 1854

freedom. Judge Paine's decision was a strong statement against slavery.

In 1854, Arthur passed his law tests and became a lawyer. Culver saw many great qualities in Arthur. Arthur worked hard, was smart, and loved the law. He soon became a partner in Culver's law firm.

In 1855, Arthur found himself fighting another **civil rights** case. He defended an African American woman named Elizabeth Jennings. Jennings had been forced off a Brooklyn, New York, streetcar reserved for white people. Arthur won $250 for Jennings.

The court victory helped change New York laws. Now, **discrimination** on New York public transportation was forbidden. African Americans were allowed to ride any streetcar they wished. Arthur became famous around New York. He was known as a defender of African American rights.

In 1857, Arthur moved to Kansas to support Free-Soilers. However, he returned to New York after just a few months.

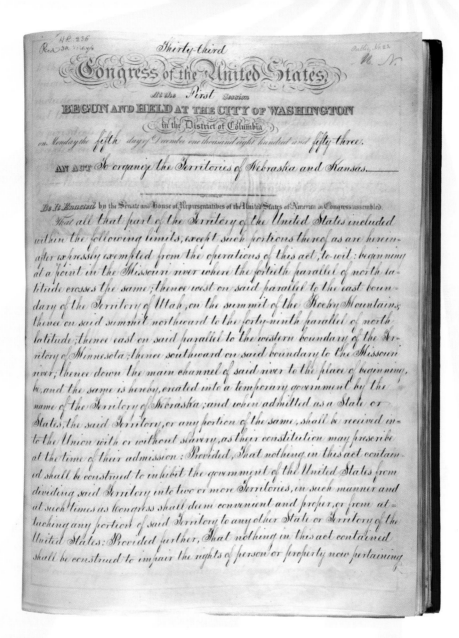

Congress passed the Kansas-Nebraska
Act in 1854. This act allowed settlers
of these territories to decide if they
wanted to legalize slavery.

Starting a Family

In 1856, Arthur started his own law practice. His office was in New York City, New York. To bring in new business, Arthur joined clubs. He loved to discuss books, politics, and fishing. Arthur made many new friends, and his business grew.

Around this time, Arthur met Ellen Lewis Herndon. Ellen was from Fredericksburg, Virginia. She was outgoing and loved to sing. She had even been trained to sing opera. Arthur and Ellen married on October 25, 1859.

Ellen Herndon Arthur

Mr. and Mrs. Arthur had a loving marriage. They eventually had three children. William Lewis was born in 1860. Sadly, he died when he was just two. Chester Alan was born in 1864. He was called Alan. Then in 1871, Ellen Herndon was born. The family called her Nelly.

Ellen Arthur

Entering Politics

Meanwhile, Arthur was growing more interested in politics. In New York, he helped form the new **Republican** Party. Arthur was not interested in holding any political offices. However, he soon attracted the attention of Republican leaders.

In 1859, Republican Edwin D. Morgan became governor of New York. He made Arthur the state engineer-in-chief with the rank of brigadier general. In 1861, the American **Civil War** began. Morgan placed Arthur in charge of giving supplies to the New York **militia**.

In 1862, Governor Morgan made Arthur the New York quartermaster general. Arthur's duties included supplying housing, food, and equipment for **Union** troops.

Arthur was an efficient leader. Commonly, the quartermaster general would have set up government-run kitchens. However, Arthur wanted to save the state money. So, he found people to bid for the work. Arthur gave the work to the person who offered the lowest price.

Governor Edwin D. Morgan

Government Work

In 1863, a **Democrat** replaced Morgan as governor of New York. Morgan and his staff lost their jobs. So, Arthur returned to his law practice. He handled many cases and became a wealthy man.

In 1868, Arthur helped Ulysses S. Grant win the presidential election. Grant rewarded Arthur in 1871. He made Arthur the collector of the New York customhouse. The customhouse employed about 1,000 workers. At the time, this was the nation's largest federal office. It collected much of the country's **tariffs**.

Arthur hired workers for the customhouse. He believed in the spoils system.

Following Arthur's appointment to customhouse collector, the *New York Times* reported, "this man during the last ten years has done more to mold the course of the Republican party in this state than any other man in the country."

Ulysses S. Grant served as president from 1869 to 1877.

So, he gave many key jobs to **Republicans**. In return, they contributed money to the Republican Party. This made the party wealthy and powerful.

Sad Days

In 1877, Rutherford B. Hayes became president. Hayes did not like the spoils system. He believed only qualified people should hold government jobs.

Rutherford B. Hayes was president from 1877 to 1881.

The next year, Arthur lost his job at the New York customhouse. He was upset because he felt he had done a great job. Despite his disappointment, Arthur returned to practicing law. And, he enthusiastically continued supporting the **Republican** Party.

At this time, Arthur was named chairman of the New York Republican Party. As chairman, he was responsible for raising money and votes for Republicans. He also spent much time socializing.

In January 1880, tragedy struck the Arthur family. Mrs. Arthur became very ill after standing outdoors in the cold. Arthur was in Albany, New York, on a business trip. He rushed home as soon as he received the news. Sadly, Ellen Arthur died of **pneumonia** on January 12.

Arthur was deeply saddened by the loss of his wife. She had been a wonderful wife and mother. After her death, Arthur had trouble working. He was also left to care for their two children alone.

Mrs. Arthur was just 42 when she died.

Vice President

To forget his sadness, Arthur focused on the upcoming **Republican National Convention**. In June 1880, the **Republicans** chose Senator-elect James A. Garfield to run for president. Arthur's party loyalty did not go unnoticed. Garfield chose Arthur as his **running mate**.

REPUBLICAN NATIONAL TICKET.

FOR PRESIDENT,
JAMES A. GARFIELD.

FOR VICE-PRESIDENT,
CHESTER A. ARTHUR.

PRESIDENTIAL ELECTORS.
ELECTORS-AT-LARGE,
SIDNEY S. WARNER.

CHARLES H. GROSVENOR.

DISTRICT ELECTORS.
ANTHONY D. BULLOCK.

ALFRED T. GOSHORN.

ROBERT E. DOAN.

WILLIAM ALLEN.

JACOB L'H. LONG.

OCTAVIUS WATERS.

WILLIAM W. McKNIGHT.

JOHN Q. A. CAMPBELL.

GEORGE W. HOLLAND.

JACOB F. BURKET.

NELSON B. SISSON.

GEORGE E. MARTIN.

MENDAL CHURCHILL.

JACOB SCROGGS.

TOBIAS A. PLANTS.

JOHN MILTON LEWIS.

NATHAN B. BILLINGSLEY.

NATHANIEL W. GOODHUE.

SAMUEL R. HOUSE.

JOEL W. TYLER.

JAMES A. GARFIELD
REPUBLICAN CANDIDATE FOR PRESIDENT

CHESTER A. ARTHUR
REPUBLICAN CANDIDATE FOR VICE PRESIDENT

A ticket is a list of candidates running together in an election.

Garfield's **Democratic** opponent was General Winfield Scott Hancock. Hancock's **running mate** was former Indiana congressman William H. English.

Arthur and Garfield spent the next few months campaigning. Then in November, they won the election! On March 4, 1881, Garfield became the twentieth US president. That day, Arthur became the nation's vice president.

Garfield did not serve long as president, however. On July 2, Charles Guiteau shot President Garfield. Guiteau was angry because he wanted Arthur to be president.

Charles Guiteau

For nearly three months, Garfield struggled to live. Then on September 19, James Garfield died. The next day at 2:15 a.m., Arthur took the oath of office. Now, he was the twenty-first US president.

The Twenty-First President

Before becoming vice president, Arthur had never been an elected official. Outside New York State, people didn't know him very well. So, many Americans believed he was unfit to be president. Now, President Arthur had to win America's trust.

In 1882, Congress wanted Arthur to approve an $18 million bill. The money would go toward improving the country's waterways. Arthur **vetoed** this expensive spending bill. But Congress passed it anyway.

Also in 1882, President Arthur signed the first act that limited **immigration**. The Chinese Exclusion Act barred the immigration of Chinese laborers for ten years. The Edmunds Anti-Polygamy Act also passed that year. This act made it illegal for a man to have more than one wife.

Arthur is called the "Father of the American Navy." This is

★ ＊
SUPREME COURT APPOINTMENTS

HORACE GRAY: 1882
SAMUEL BLATCHFORD: 1882

because as president, Arthur improved the US Navy. In 1883, Congress set aside money to create the nation's first all-steel ships.

In 1883, President Arthur signed the nation's first **civil service** law. The Pendleton Civil Service Act is still in effect today. It requires the federal government to hire people based on ability, not political party.

Also that year, Congress passed a law that lowered **tariffs**. However, President Arthur had wanted to lower tariffs by a much larger percentage. He did not believe this new law would do enough to improve the **economy**.

After he became president, Arthur learned his kidneys weren't working correctly. He had Bright's disease. But he kept his illness a secret. Arthur did not want people to think he was too sick to lead the nation.

The Chinese Exclusion Act

Arthur took vacations so he could rest. During a trip to Florida, Arthur caught a fever. This made his condition worse.

Despite his illness, Arthur loved to entertain in the White House. He disliked being alone. Arthur enjoyed dances and fancy dinners. When dinner was over, he urged friends to stay. After they left, Arthur often worked late into the night.

Arthur's sister Mary Arthur McElroy acted as White House hostess. She also took care of Arthur's young daughter, Nelly. By then, his son Alan was attending college in Princeton, New Jersey.

Every year, President Arthur's popularity grew. He did what he thought was best for the country. However, some of his ideas were not what the **Republicans** wanted. They did not nominate him to run for president in the 1884 election.

——— Pendleton Civil ———
Service Act

In summer 1883, Arthur (*seated, center*) traveled to Yellowstone National Park. He camped, rode horses, and went fishing there.

PRESIDENT ARTHUR'S CABINET

ONE TERM
September 20, 1881–March 4, 1885

★ **STATE:** James G. Blaine
Frederick T. Frelinghuysen (from December 19, 1881)

★ **TREASURY:** William Windom
Charles J. Folger (from November 14, 1881)
Walter Q. Gresham (from September 24, 1884)
Hugh McCulloch (from October 31, 1884)

★ **WAR:** Robert Todd Lincoln

★ **NAVY:** William Henry Hunt
William Eaton Chandler (from April 17, 1882)

★ **ATTORNEY GENERAL:** Wayne MacVeagh
Benjamin H. Brewster (from January 3, 1882)

★ **INTERIOR:** Samuel Jordan Kirkwood
Henry M. Teller (from April 17, 1882)

President Chester Arthur

Arthur Goes Home

Arthur accepted the party's decision. He knew that he was too sick to be president. When his term ended, Arthur returned to his New York home.

Publisher Alexander K. McClure said of Arthur, "No man ever entered the Presidency so profoundly and widely distrusted, and no one ever retired . . . more generally respected."

Back in New York, Arthur tried to rebuild his law practice. But he lacked the energy to work. He also entertained less. On November 18, 1886, Chester Arthur died. He was just 57 years old.

Arthur is remembered as an honest man. He worked hard for the American people. Arthur believed in and fought for the rights of all people.

At first, many people had felt Arthur was unfit to become president. But he worked hard to earn their trust. Chester Arthur proved he could be a good leader for America.

Arthur is buried in Rural Cemetery in Albany, New York.

BRANCHES OF GOVERNMENT

The US government is divided into three branches. They are the executive, legislative, and judicial branches. This division is called a separation of powers. Each branch has some power over the others. This is called a system of checks and balances.

★ EXECUTIVE BRANCH

The executive branch enforces laws. It is made up of the president, the vice president, and the president's cabinet. The president represents the United States around the world. He or she oversees relations with other countries and signs treaties. The president signs bills into law and appoints officials and federal judges. He or she also leads the military and manages government workers.

★ LEGISLATIVE BRANCH

The legislative branch makes laws, maintains the military, and regulates trade. It also has the power to declare war. This branch consists of the Senate and the House of Representatives. Together, these two houses make up Congress. Each state has two senators. A state's population determines the number of representatives it has.

★ JUDICIAL BRANCH

The judicial branch interprets laws. It consists of district courts, courts of appeals, and the Supreme Court. District courts try cases. If a person disagrees with a trial's outcome, he or she may appeal. If a court of appeals supports the ruling, a person may appeal to the Supreme Court. The Supreme Court also makes sure that laws follow the US Constitution.

THE PRESIDENT ★

★ QUALIFICATIONS FOR OFFICE

To be president, a person must meet three requirements. A candidate must be at least 35 years old and a natural-born US citizen. He or she must also have lived in the United States for at least 14 years.

★ ELECTORAL COLLEGE

The US presidential election is an indirect election. Voters from each state choose electors to represent them in the Electoral College. The number of electors from each state is based on the state's population. Each elector has one electoral vote. Electors are pledged to cast their vote for the candidate who receives the highest number of popular votes in their state. A candidate must receive the majority of Electoral College votes to win.

★ TERM OF OFFICE

Each president may be elected to two four-year terms. Sometimes, a president may only be elected once. This happens if he or she served more than two years of the previous president's term.

The presidential election is held on the Tuesday after the first Monday in November. The president is sworn in on January 20 of the following year. At that time, he or she takes the oath of office:

> *I do solemnly swear (or affirm) that I will faithfully execute the office of President of the United States, and will to the best of my ability, preserve, protect and defend the Constitution of the United States.*

LINE OF SUCCESSION

The Presidential Succession Act of 1947 defines who becomes president if the president cannot serve. The vice president is first in the line of succession. Next are the Speaker of the House and the President Pro Tempore of the Senate. If none of these individuals is able to serve, the office falls to the president's cabinet members. They would take office in the order in which each department was created:

Secretary of State

Secretary of the Treasury

Secretary of Defense

Attorney General

Secretary of the Interior

Secretary of Agriculture

Secretary of Commerce

Secretary of Labor

Secretary of Health and Human Services

Secretary of Housing and Urban Development

Secretary of Transportation

Secretary of Energy

Secretary of Education

Secretary of Veterans Affairs

Secretary of Homeland Security

While in office, the president receives a salary of $400,000 each year. He or she lives in the White House and has 24-hour Secret Service protection.

The president may travel on a Boeing 747 jet called Air Force One. The airplane can accommodate 76 passengers. It has kitchens, a dining room, sleeping areas, and a conference room. It also has fully equipped offices with the latest communications systems. Air Force One can fly halfway around the world before needing to refuel. It can even refuel in flight!

Air Force One

If the president wishes to travel by car, he or she uses Cadillac One. It has been modified with heavy armor and communications systems. The president takes

Cadillac One

Cadillac One along when visiting other countries if secure transportation will be needed.

The president also travels on a helicopter called Marine One. Like the presidential car, Marine One accompanies the president when traveling abroad if necessary.

Sometimes, the president needs to get away and relax with family and friends. Camp David is the official presidential retreat. It is located in the cool, wooded mountains of Maryland. The US Navy maintains the retreat, and the US Marine Corps keeps it secure. The camp offers swimming, tennis, golf, and hiking.

When the president leaves office, he or she receives lifetime Secret Service protection. He or she also receives a yearly pension of $207,800 and funding for office space, supplies, and staff.

Marine One

George Washington

Abraham Lincoln

Theodore Roosevelt

	PRESIDENT	PARTY	TOOK OFFICE
1	George Washington	None	April 30, 1789
2	John Adams	Federalist	March 4, 1797
3	Thomas Jefferson	Democratic-Republican	March 4, 1801
4	James Madison	Democratic-Republican	March 4, 1809
5	James Monroe	Democratic-Republican	March 4, 1817
6	John Quincy Adams	Democratic-Republican	March 4, 1825
7	Andrew Jackson	Democrat	March 4, 1829
8	Martin Van Buren	Democrat	March 4, 1837
9	William H. Harrison	Whig	March 4, 1841
10	John Tyler	Whig	April 6, 1841
11	James K. Polk	Democrat	March 4, 1845
12	Zachary Taylor	Whig	March 5, 1849
13	Millard Fillmore	Whig	July 10, 1850
14	Franklin Pierce	Democrat	March 4, 1853
15	James Buchanan	Democrat	March 4, 1857
16	Abraham Lincoln	Republican	March 4, 1861
17	Andrew Johnson	Democrat	April 15, 1865
18	Ulysses S. Grant	Republican	March 4, 1869
19	Rutherford B. Hayes	Republican	March 3, 1877

THEIR TERMS ★

LEFT OFFICE	TERMS SERVED	VICE PRESIDENT
March 4, 1797	Two	John Adams
March 4, 1801	One	Thomas Jefferson
March 4, 1809	Two	Aaron Burr, George Clinton
March 4, 1817	Two	George Clinton, Elbridge Gerry
March 4, 1825	Two	Daniel D. Tompkins
March 4, 1829	One	John C. Calhoun
March 4, 1837	Two	John C. Calhoun, Martin Van Buren
March 4, 1841	One	Richard M. Johnson
April 4, 1841	Died During First Term	John Tyler
March 4, 1845	Completed Harrison's Term	Office Vacant
March 4, 1849	One	George M. Dallas
July 9, 1850	Died During First Term	Millard Fillmore
March 4, 1853	Completed Taylor's Term	Office Vacant
March 4, 1857	One	William R.D. King
March 4, 1861	One	John C. Breckinridge
April 15, 1865	Served One Term, Died During Second Term	Hannibal Hamlin, Andrew Johnson
March 4, 1869	Completed Lincoln's Second Term	Office Vacant
March 4, 1877	Two	Schuyler Colfax, Henry Wilson
March 4, 1881	One	William A. Wheeler

Franklin D. Roosevelt

John F. Kennedy

Ronald Reagan

	PRESIDENT	PARTY	TOOK OFFICE
20	James A. Garfield	Republican	March 4, 1881
21	Chester Arthur	Republican	September 20, 1881
22	Grover Cleveland	Democrat	March 4, 1885
23	Benjamin Harrison	Republican	March 4, 1889
24	Grover Cleveland	Democrat	March 4, 1893
25	William McKinley	Republican	March 4, 1897
26	Theodore Roosevelt	Republican	September 14, 1901
27	William Taft	Republican	March 4, 1909
28	Woodrow Wilson	Democrat	March 4, 1913
29	Warren G. Harding	Republican	March 4, 1921
30	Calvin Coolidge	Republican	August 3, 1923
31	Herbert Hoover	Republican	March 4, 1929
32	Franklin D. Roosevelt	Democrat	March 4, 1933
33	Harry S. Truman	Democrat	April 12, 1945
34	Dwight D. Eisenhower	Republican	January 20, 1953
35	John F. Kennedy	Democrat	January 20, 1961

LEFT OFFICE	TERMS SERVED	VICE PRESIDENT
September 19, 1881	Died During First Term	Chester Arthur
March 4, 1885	Completed Garfield's Term	Office Vacant
March 4, 1889	One	Thomas A. Hendricks
March 4, 1893	One	Levi P. Morton
March 4, 1897	One	Adlai E. Stevenson
September 14, 1901	Served One Term, Died During Second Term	Garret A. Hobart, Theodore Roosevelt
March 4, 1909	Completed McKinley's Second Term, Served One Term	Office Vacant, Charles Fairbanks
March 4, 1913	One	James S. Sherman
March 4, 1921	Two	Thomas R. Marshall
August 2, 1923	Died During First Term	Calvin Coolidge
March 4, 1929	Completed Harding's Term, Served One Term	Office Vacant, Charles Dawes
March 4, 1933	One	Charles Curtis
April 12, 1945	Served Three Terms, Died During Fourth Term	John Nance Garner, Henry A. Wallace, Harry S. Truman
January 20, 1953	Completed Roosevelt's Fourth Term, Served One Term	Office Vacant, Alben Barkley
January 20, 1961	Two	Richard Nixon
November 22, 1963	Died During First Term	Lyndon B. Johnson

Barack Obama

	PRESIDENT	PARTY	TOOK OFFICE
36	Lyndon B. Johnson	Democrat	November 22, 1963
37	Richard Nixon	Republican	January 20, 1969
38	Gerald Ford	Republican	August 9, 1974
39	Jimmy Carter	Democrat	January 20, 1977
40	Ronald Reagan	Republican	January 20, 1981
41	George H.W. Bush	Republican	January 20, 1989
42	Bill Clinton	Democrat	January 20, 1993
43	George W. Bush	Republican	January 20, 2001
44	Barack Obama	Democrat	January 20, 2009
45	Donald Trump	Republican	January 20, 2017

★ PRESIDENTS MATH GAME ★

Have fun with this presidents math game! First, study the list above and memorize each president's name and number. Then, use math to figure out which president completes each equation below.

1. Grover Cleveland + Chester Arthur = ?

2. Chester Arthur + Abraham Lincoln = ?

3. William McKinley − Chester Arthur = ?

Answers: **1.** George W. Bush (22 + 21 = 43)
2. Richard Nixon (21 + 16 = 37)
3. James Madison (25 − 21 = 4)

LEFT OFFICE	TERMS SERVED	VICE PRESIDENT
January 20, 1969	Completed Kennedy's Term, Served One Term	Office Vacant, Hubert H. Humphrey
August 9, 1974	Completed First Term, Resigned During Second Term	Spiro T. Agnew, Gerald Ford
January 20, 1977	Completed Nixon's Second Term	Nelson A. Rockefeller
January 20, 1981	One	Walter Mondale
January 20, 1989	Two	George H.W. Bush
January 20, 1993	One	Dan Quayle
January 20, 2001	Two	Al Gore
January 20, 2009	Two	Dick Cheney
January 20, 2017	Two	Joe Biden
		Mike Pence

★ WRITE TO THE PRESIDENT ★

You may write to the president at:

**The White House
1600 Pennsylvania Avenue NW
Washington, DC 20500**

You may email the president at:

www.whitehouse.gov/contact

★ GLOSSARY ★

apprentice—a person who learns a trade or a craft from a skilled worker.

assassinate—to murder a very important person, usually for political reasons.

civil rights—rights that protect people from unequal treatment or discrimination.

civil service—the part of the government that is responsible for matters not covered by the military, the courts, or the law.

civil war—a war between groups in the same country. The United States of America and the Confederate States of America fought a civil war from 1861 to 1865.

Democrat—a member of the Democratic political party. When Chester Arthur was president, Democrats supported farmers and landowners.

discrimination (dihs-krih-muh-NAY-shuhn)—unfair treatment based on factors such as a person's race, religion, or gender.

economy—the way a nation uses its money, goods, and natural resources.

immigration—entry into another country to live.

militia (muh-LIH-shuh)—a group of citizens trained for war or emergencies.

pneumonia (nu-MOH-nyuh)—a disease that affects the lungs and may cause fever, coughing, or difficulty breathing.

Republican—a member of the Republican political party. When Chester Arthur was president, Republicans supported business and strong government.

Republican National Convention—a national meeting held every four years during which the Republican Party chooses its candidates for president and vice president.

running mate—a candidate running for a lower-rank position on an election ticket, especially the candidate for vice president.

tariff—the taxes a government puts on imported or exported goods.

Union—relating to the states that remained in the United States during the American Civil War.

veto—the right of one member of a decision-making group to stop an action by the group. In the US government, the president can veto bills passed by Congress. But Congress can override the president's veto if two-thirds of its members vote to do so.

ONLINE RESOURCES

Booklinks
NONFICTION NETWORK
FREE! ONLINE NONFICTION RESOURCES

To learn more about Chester Arthur, please visit **abdobooklinks.com** or scan this QR code. These links are routinely monitored and updated to provide the most current information available.

★ INDEX ★